# The Coming War Over Palestine

*By*

DAN GILBERT, LL. D., Litt. D.

GENERAL BOOK AND BIBLE HOUSE
4800 South Hoover Street
Los Angeles 37, California

ISBN: 978-2-925369-61-5
Printed in the USA.

# CONTENTS

## PALESTINE: "THE HEART THROB OF HISTORY"

The Holy Land is the "heart throb of history"—both secular and sacred.

What goes on "inside Palestine" reveals the future course of world history. It also reveals the fulfilment of the Divine Plan which culminates in the Second Coming of Christ.

Every student of Bible Prophecy keeps his eyes upon the Jews. By watching what they are doing, we may know *what* God is going to do—and *when* He is going to do it!

This was precisely the answer given by Christ when His disciples asked the question: "What shall be the sign of thy coming, and of the end of the world?" (Matthew 24:3)

The Lord explained, "Now learn a parable of the fig tree; when his branch is yet tender, and putteth forth leaves, ye know that summer is nigh."

Even the elementary student of Prophecy knows that "the fig tree means the Jews." In Jeremiah 24: 1-8, as well as elsewhere in Old and New Testaments, God makes "figs to be symbols of the Jews."

When the Prophetic student wants to know "what time it is according to the Biblical timetable," he consults God's ancient timepiece: the Jew. He surveys what is going on among the people and in the land of Israel. He seeks answers to the questions: Is the fig tree beginning to put forth leaves? Is the fig tree budding?

God uses many figures and symbols to set forth His great prophetic truth regarding the future of the people and land of Israel. But none is more significant and instructive than "the fig tree"—unless it is the familiar "dry bones" of Ezekiel!

Ezekiel was transported by the Lord and deposited "in the midst of the valley which was full of bones . . . and, lo, they were very dry." He was asked if these bones could live. Humbly and sensibly he replied: "O Lord God, thou knowest."

"The valley full of very dry bones" is a realistic picture of the condition of Israel through many centuries. Israel was saying then, as her spokesmen have wailed incessantly ever since, "Our bones are dried, and our hope is lost." But help comes from heaven!

The bones are literally resurrected and *reassembled*: "there was a noise, and behold a shaking, and the bones came together, bone to his bone. And when I beheld, lo, the sinews and the fleseh came up upon them, and the skin covered them above: but there was no breath in them." At God's Word to the four winds, "the breath came into them, and they lived, and stood up upon their feet, an exceeding great army."

In matchless vision, Ezekiel saw before him the glorious future of Israel: "Thus saith the Lord God; Behold, O my people, I will open your graves, and cause you to come up out of your graves, and bring you into the land of Israel. And ye shall know that I am the Lord, when I have opened your graves, O my people, and brought you up out of your graves." (Ezekiel 37:12-13)

The Second World War was the final result of the "saber-rattling" indulged in by the war lords of Germany and Japan. Empty-headed optimists might stick their heads in the sands of ignorance, but thoughtful observers knew that war was inevitable—when they heard the sword-rattling of Hitler and Hirohito, way back in the middle nineteen-thirties.

Scoffers may laugh, but believers of God's Word know that the Second Coming of Christ is not far off—now that the earth itself is beginning to tremble with the "shaking of Ezekiel's bones"!

Palestine has become the center of the stage of world history. The international spotlight is upon the land of Abraham.

Washington, London, and Moscow have focused their attention upon "the navel of the earth."

# BRITAIN'S BROKEN PROMISES

Throughout September and October, 1945, the clouds of bloody conflict were gathering over the Holy Land. Newspaper headlines reported rumblings and grumblings throughout the Arab world.

Why?

On August 31, President Truman laid before the British government the idea that 100,000 Jewish refugees from Europe ought to be admitted into Palestine.

Following the well-practiced procedure, which they always resort to when any move is made to bring more Jews into Palestine, the Arabs launched a "war of nerves," with attendant threats of bloodshed and violence. There was just enough rioting in Palestine to implement their campaign of intimidation.

By the middle of November, the "crisis" was reached. A group of newsmen in Washington, D. C., sat outside while important government officials were huddled in conference. Out of the conference would come the word: Peace or Bloodshed for Palestine!

The word finally was released and it was—Peace!

Around the globe, newspaper headlines heralded: ALL QUIET ON THE PALESTINIAN FRONT.

But the echo of the newsboys' shouting of these headlines, "ALL QUIET IN PALESTINE," had hardly faded away, before the "quiet" was shattered by "NEW VIOLENCE IN PALESTINE." The clever compromises of Attlee have led to nothing except new outbreaks of violence involving both Jews and Arabs. How long will it take our "democratic statesmen" to learn that peace cannot come to men or nations through a policy of disobedience to God?

The tension in the Holy Land has relaxed. The "clouds of bloody conflict" have lifted.

How? Why?

Once more Great Britain and America have "given in to the Arabs." We have gone through another humiliating "retreat." President Truman has "withdrawn" his request that Britain permit an additional 100,000 homeless Jews to *go home* to the place provided for them by God Himself.

A "new arrangement on Palestine" has been entered into by President Truman and Prime Minister Attlee. There is to be an Anglo-American "Committee of Inquiry" to "look into the whole problem of European Jews in Palestine."

But, in the meantime, "there is to be no *increase* of Jewish migration to Palestine." We are told, "it is hoped to maintain the present rate of 1500 permits per month, that is all."

"Peace in Palestine" has been purchased at the price of humiliation and dishonor for Britain and America. We are now the most powerful combination of military powers on the face of the earth. We have just completed the exercise of our military might to overthrow God-denying tyranny in Germany and Japan. Yet, in the face of Arab threats of violence, we have failed to obey God's Command and establish His people in the place where His Word declares that they belong.

Assuredly, no one wants bloodshed—at any time. But America was founded on the principle that death is to be preferred to slavery. America waged this great war to "carry the four freedoms to the ends of the earth." But there is no freedom for the Jews—no freedom even to go to the home which the Lord has designated for them.

The controverysy over Palestine is not merely a contest between Arabs and Jews: with America and Britain sitting on the sidelines as "umpires." The "future of Palestine" is not to be decided by the Allied nations at any "peace conference" or session of any "board of inquiry." God has already settled it—beyond the power of man to alter. The British government may talk generously of "dividing the land" between the Jews and Arabs. But God has already declared that every inch of it belongs to His ancient people. Their "deed of ownership and possession" bears Heavenly credentials.

The only question for America and Britain to settle is this:

Will we uphold the "title" to Palestine which the Jews have received from God Himself? Will we obey God's Divine decree that the Jews shall be reassembled in Palestine? Or will we—along with the heathen nations—defy Him?

Only woe and disaster can come upon any nation which obstructs the program of God. Every American citizen ought to pray that our beloved nation shall not bring upon herself the judgment of God by conspiring with other nations to stand in the way of the fulfillment of His Plan for His people.

No person can believe the Bible and deny that it is God's purpose to reassemble the Jews in Palestine prior to the Return of Christ. Yet, the very leaders of so-called Christian nations are joining with the unbelievers in attempting to block and defeat God's Purpose!

The Lord says clearly, "I will gather the remnant of my flock out of all countries whither I have driven them, and will bring them again to their folds: and they shall be fruitful and increase. And I will set up shepherds over them which shall feed them and they shall fear no more, nor be dismayed, neither shall they be lacking, saith the Lord." (Jer. 23: 3-4)

Again, the Lord declares of "my people Israel": "I will cause them to return to the land that I gave to their fathers, and they shall possess it."

God declares unto the nations His unalterable purpose to gather the Jews in Palestine: "I will say to the north, give up; and to the south, keep not back: bring my sons from far, and my daughters from the ends of the earth." (Isa. 43:6)

Again God asserts, "Hear the word of the Lord, O ye nations, and declare it in the isles afar off, and say, He that scattered Israel will gather him, and keep him, as a shepherd doth his flock."

The Lord commands the nations to *bring* the Jews from the ends of the earth to Palestine. Yet the very Jewish refugees who have flocked to the borders of their own land are now kept out by the military power of nations which were founded upon God's Word!

In the 54th chapter of Isaiah, God warns that there will be

nations which will conspire together to block the Jews out of their own domain, but He declares, "whosoever shall gather together against thee shall fall for thy sake."

But all the military power of the United Nations cannot keep the Jews permanently out of Palestine. The Lord will settle them there, despite all that men and nations may do to thwart His Purpose.

Before the "fig tree" could bud, the climate and soil must be favorable to this development. The sap must flow in accordance with Nature's recurrent miracle.

Preparatory to their reoccupation of Palestine, the Lord has worked to create new life and unity in Israel. Only a few decades ago, Israel was without either hope or vision. In 1882, a world-renowned Jewish leader, Dr. Leo Pinsker, issued a highly-publicized *Appeal* to his people. He urged them to turn their backs upon God and His promise to provide them with a restored home in Palestine. He counseled them, instead, to seek a destiny of their own—rejecting the one which the Lord has promised.

Dr. Pinsker wrote, "We must, above all, not dream of restoring ancient Judea. We must not attach ourselves to the place where our political life was once violently interrupted and destroyed. The goal of our present endeavors must not be the 'Holy Land' but a land of our own."

But despite this kind of defeatist propaganda, new hopes and new vision have been kindled in the hearts of millions of Jews during the last several decades. The Jews of the earth have come to "look homeward"—not with despair, disillusion, and hopelessness; but with eagerness and expectancy.

In 1897, the first Zionist Congress was held at Basel, Switzerland. The platform adopted had the slogan: "Zionism aims at establishing for the Jewish people a publicly and legally assured home in Palestine."

Through the Zionist movement, the Jews of the world have been brought together, the "scattered bones" of dead hopes and disunity have been integrated in a revived and revitalized racial purpose. Through Zionism, the Jews of the world have been made one in hope and aspiration; eventually, they will be made one in geographical location!

## THE TIME OF JACOB'S BETRAYAL

The Zionist aim of regaining Palestine for the Jews was enthusiastically endorsed by the British government. In the famous Balfour declaration, it was asserted: "His Majesty's government view with favor the establishment in Palestine of a national home for the Jewish people, and will use their best efforts to facilitate the attainment of this object."

On December 9, 1917, General Allenby marched into Jeruaslem. Scarcely a shot was fired. In perfect fulfillment of Isaiah 31, the city bore no wounds or scars of conflict.

In March, 1918, the Jewish flag was unfurled atop the Tower of David. General Allenby officially proclaimed the establishment of a *Jewish state*.

Yet in November, 1945, the Jews are barred from Palestine! Millions of them are hungry and cold, wanderers over the wartorn wastelands of Europe, because the guns of the British army forbid them to go to their own land! Well may the reader ask: What happened in the intervening years? When the Jewish state was proclaimed in Palestine, the Zionist dream of the ages seemed to have been realized. What happened to transform that "dream-come-true" into a mirage —or, more accurately, a nightmare?

The story of the past 25 years makes sad reading—of Jewish hopes raised heaven-high, only to be dashed into the tearstained sands of bitter disappointment and despair.

On May 24, 1920, the League of Nations formally ratified Britain's "mandate" over Palestine. The League of Nations, it should be recalled, was the organization which was supposed to "rule the earth in peace and righteousness." The League was supposed to guarantee that the world would be kept "safe for democracy" and that Palestine would be kept safe for the Jews. Hence, when the League of Nations officially "underwrote" the British program of "Palestine-for-the-Jews," it was widely proclaimed that the hour of "Jacob's rejoicing" had come.

(But the Scriptures tell of the time of "Jacob's trouble." This is the Age of the Gentiles. There is no "rejoicing for Jacob" under Gentile rule.)

When Herbert Samuel became Governor of Palestine, the Jews had one of their own in authority. Back of this authority was the might and power of the British Empire. And back of the British Empire was the might and power of the League of Nations—plus the United States! While keeping out of the League of Nations, America never withheld either financial or military support from the British!

Jews have a tradition of taking pride in their homes; and once they were established in their "international homeland," they proceeded to make "deserts into orchards." Palestine was made to bud and blossom after the manner of the long-retarded "fig tree." In the middle of the Depression, the *Sunday Express*, published in London, reported of Palestine: "Look at Palestine! No crisis there—no unemployment. In four years the customs receipts are up three hundred percent, the value of imports doubled, the investment capital trebled. New towns shoot up. . . . The Promised Land is an industrial state. Once more it flows with milk and honey."

When the Jews moved into Palestine following World War I, few of them would have anticipated any serious trouble with the Arabs twenty years later.

The Arabs had Palestine from 637 A. D. until the Turks took the land away from them in 1516. They appeared completely indifferent when the British took the territory from the Turks in 1918 and proceeded to turn it over to the Jews afterwards.

Anxious to avoid trouble, the Zionist leaders met with the Arab rulers and arranged to purchase the tracts of land which the latter claimed to own. The Arabs seemed eager to sell—at a price estimated to be six times the actual value of the land! Heavily financed by Jewish interests throughout the world, the Zionist directors did not haggle over the figure, but cheerfully paid the price requested.

Obviously, the Arabs had little, if any, prevision of the

manner in which the ingenious and industrious Jews would promptly convert Palestine into an earthly paradise. By developing the country industrially as well as agriculturally, the Jews were able to create for themselves a standard of living which excited the envy of the poverty-stricken Arabs.

The result was a growing campaign of agitation and murmurings on the part of the Arabs. In his book on *Palestine,* Harry Rimmer gives an example of just how crude and pathetic is the Arab "argument" that the Jews have no right to occupy the land. When the Arabs demanded possession of the very tracts which they had legally sold, the Jews would ask, "What price do you offer to buy it back?"

The Arabs would answer, "We have no money. But it is our land, and has been for six hundred years."

The Jews would reply, "But you sold it."

The Arabs would weakly retort, "The sale was a mistake and we regret it. Now we intend to take the land back."

Dr. Rimmer declares that "for every Jew who has returned to Palestine, six Arabs have immigrated into the land, and it is these immigrant Moslems from Syria, Iraq, Trans-Jordania and Arabia who are causing the disturbance."

Led by professional trouble-makers, a lawless mob of Arab vagrants and vagabonds roam the country, preying upon the hard-working Jewish inhabitants, and staging special demonstrations of violence whenever it is suggested that Jewish immigration should be resumed on any sizeable scale.

This Arab mob is without military equipment or training. Its worst "acts of terrorism" consist of breaking store windows and assaulting unprotected Jewish citizens on the streets or in their homes. Yet the world has been led to believe that it is fear of this mob that has caused the proud and powerful British government to break its word to the Jews. As everyone knows, it was more than five years ago that the British issued a "white paper" suspending the Balfour Declaration and its provision for unrestricted Jewish immigation into Palestine. Under the terms of that suspension, which is still in effect, Jewish immigration is virtually prohibited, except for a "token trickle" of 1500 or fewer "permits" per month. When President Truman suggested immediate admission of 100,000 European Jews into Palestine, the Arabs launched a feeble demonstration of "window-breaking" and "civilian-assault." The contemptible attitude of the Arab mob has consistently been: keep the Jews out—or else! The Arab leadership has made no effort to base its position on either law or ethics; it has simply made veiled threats of terrorism.

In his statement on Palestine, refusing to accede to the Truman request, Ernest Bevin, the British foreign secretary, raised the feeblest of scarecrows. He fearfully suggested that the 90,000,000 Moslems in India might "get stirred up," if the Arabs were antagonized in Palestine by an increase in Jewish immigration.

But, strangely, the British have no hesitancy in "stirring up the Moslems" in other parts of the world. At the very time that Mr. Bevin announced the policy of giving in to the Moslem demands in Palestine, British military forces were bombing and shelling the Moslems of Indonesia, fighting for independence!

The British are quite willing to use bayonets and bombing planes upon the rebelling Moslems of Java! Why, then, are they unwilling to use force upon the Arabs? In no part of the world, except in Palestine, do we find the British backing down in the face of native uprisings, permiting a mob of Moslems to defy the authority of the British crown.

Obviously, there is more to the Palestinian situation than appears on the surface. There is a deeper conflict than the superficial one between Arabs on the one side and Jews and their supposed "British protectors" on the other side.

England, assuredly, is not afraid of the Arabs, who are destitute of mechanized military equipment of any kind. A schoolboy could figure out that there must be a power behind the Arab revolt—a power which the British fear to offend. There must be a greater influence in world affairs than that wielded by the Arabs, *which dictates that the Jews shall be kept out of their own country.*

The identity of this "greater influence in world affairs" becomes apparent when we examine the distressing record of Uncle Sam in failing to make effective his loudly-spoken championship of the Jews, and of their right to Palestine.

## THE YALTA "DOUBLE-CROSS"

In 1944, the platforms of both the Republican and Democratic parties called for *immediate* and *unrestricted* Jewish immigration into Palestine. Both party platforms also called for the full and unqualified recognition of Palestine as an international homeland for the Jews.

The Roosevelt-Truman ticket was elected on that platform, which was reinforced by the speeches and statements of the candidates, pledging that this nation would champion the cause of full possession of Palestine by and for the Jews.

When President Truman suggested a fractional fulfillment of a tiny part of this pledge—the admission of a mere 100,000 Jews to Palestine—the King of Arabia darkly hinted that he had a "secret agreement" in writing from the late President Roosevelt, guaranteeing that the Jews would be kept out of Palestine (until the Arabs wanted them there, which would be no sooner than the sands of the desert grow cold!)

Later, when challenged, the Arab King proudly produced the letter. The White House did not deny its authenticity. Written about the time of the Yalta Conference with Stalin, the letter gave assurances that there would be no increase in Jewish immigration without prior consultation and agreement with the Arabs.

The "timing" of the letter clearly reveals the "hidden hand" which is exerting every possible pressure to block the Jews out of their own country. That "hidden hand," working so deftly behind the scenes, is of course the agile paw of the Russian bear!

All analysts are agreed that the Yalta Conference represented the "greatest of Stalin's diplomatic triumphs." President Roosevelt went to Yalta seeking two things from Stalin: (1) the full and faithful participation of Russia in the United Nations organization; and (2) active participation of Russia in the war against Japan. With some delays and qualifications, Stalin acceded to both requests. But, as always, his price was high. First, he exacted a promise of a post-war loan of nine billion dollars. Second, he required that the Arab king should be given "assurance" that the program for making Palestine a Jewish state should be thwarted.

One of the most cunning and calculated, as well as far-reaching, of all Bolshevik projects is the winning of the good will of the so-called Moslem world. Sunk in superstition, ignorance, and squalor, the whole Mohammedan "belt" stretching from Africa across India to the Dutch East Indies and the Pacific Ocean represents a seething mass of humanity "ripe for revolt." The Nazis did their best to arouse and inflame the Moslem peoples against the white man. But while they produced some flare-ups, they were unable to create a full-sized explosion.

The strategy of every subversive movement—Communist, Fascist, or Nazi—is to stir up any downtrodden and underprivileged people. The stirring of race and religious and class war is a specialty.

Soviet Russia has now boldly aligned herself on the side of the whole Moslem world. In revolting against the Dutch and British, the Indonesians openly appealed to Moscow for reinforcements. Probably there is no way that Russia could get military supplies to the native rebels, but the issuance of the appeal is the strongest evidence that the Communist propaganda agents have secretly promised Soviet support of the attempted revolution.

Apparently, however, Stalin has no intention of "going to bat" for the Indonesians, as he did for the Arabs. Naturally, we cannot know just what kind or how much pressure he put upon the late President Roosevelt to cause him to side with the Arabs in contradiction to his plain promises to the Jews. But it must have been tremendous—and timed so as to take full advantage of the situation which prevailed at the Yalta Conference, wherein the Presient looked to Russia for aid both in setting up the United Nations organization and in crushing Japan.

In any appraisal of the president's action, historians of the future will take into account the fact that Mr. Roosevelt's whole heart and life were set upon the achievement of a world organization which would realize the dream which faded out with the League of Nations. If he agreed to the Russian-Arab demand, in contradiction to his promise to the Jews, it was doubtless because he felt that this was not too high a price to pay for full Soviet concurrence in the United Nations' program. We say this neither in condemnation nor justification of the President's action—but only in the effort to attain full understanding of his motive. Of course, as a believer in the Biblical standard of ethics, no Christian can approve of breaking one's promise, for any purpose, under any condition, to achieve any conceivable objective.

## THE ARAB-SOVIET ALLIANCE

It is the Purpose and Program of God to resettle and re-assemble the Jews in Palestine as this Age comes to a close. Christ referred to this process as the budding of the "fig tree." Ezekiel referred to it as a relocation, restoration, and resurrection of the dry bones. Amos referred to it as a "re-construction" of the tabernacle of David: "In that day I will raise up the tabernacle of David that is fallen, and close up the breaches thereof: and I will raise up his ruins, and I will build it as in the days of old." (Amos 9:11)

Prophecy teaches that an anti-God combine of nations shall oppose the Divine purpose and program for Israel. The rallying slogan of the godless forces shall be: "Come, and let us cut them off from being a nation; that the name of Israel be no more in remembrance." (Ps. 83:4)

Ezekiel tells of the resettling of the Jews in Palestine. He also tells of the terrible enemy, the dreadful adversary that shall descend upon the Holy Land "to take a spoil, and to take a prey."

Ezekiel names the "aggressor nation": the arch-enemy of Israel, which organizes a great military force to invade and despoil the land of Palestine.

That nation is *Russia*—not *Arabia*.

In his authoritative book, *Russian Events in the Light of Bible Prophecy*, Dr. Louis S. Bauman gives many pages of ironclad proofs that the *Gog* of Ezekiel 38 and 39—the arch-aggressor against the land and people of Israel—is the Moscow dictator. However, as Dr. Scofield observed many years ago, all Bible scholars have always been agreed that *Gog* is Russia. Even a child reading Ezekiel 38 and 39 would readily recognize that the invader of Israel's land—who "comes from his place out of the north parts"—is the Bolshevik grizzly! For, Russia has the only avowedly atheistic, anti-God government in the world; and Ezekiel describes the aggressor against

Palestine as being a nation which "is against God" and which "God is against."

While the Scriptures plainly instruct that the coming "battle over Palestine" will feature Russian aggression against God and the people of God and the land of the people of God, the Soviet strategists have headlined the developing struggle as a clash between "Arabs and Jews."

Communist promoters and propagandists are experts at carrying on their subversive activity behind the "false front" of innocent-sounding organizations. Usually, they carry on their sabotage of American industry behind the mask of a phoney "labor movement" of one kind or another. Uniformly, they pursue their destructive political purposes under the guise of some sort of "mobilization for democracy." To supply a shield and cover, under which they seek to sabotage the fulfillment of God's purpose and program in Palestine, they have sponsored and financed the much-discussed *Arab League of Nations.*

A foreign correspondent of established reputation has given this illuminating expose of the so-called Arab League. He writes, "Despite cunning attempts at camouflage, the guiding hand of Moscow is evident in its every maneuver. The Arab League carries on international negotiations according to the familiar pattern of a communist-controlled C. I. O. union. There is much bluffing and blustering. There are "demonstrations" with sporadic outbursts of violence. There are ultimatums laid down with appropriate displays of 'toughness' and of threats of 'worse things to come'.

"This kind of 'bargaining' requires constant practice. The British have cultivated the art for centuries. But the Bolsheviks have always excelled in this field—possibly because of their unmitigated unscrupulousness. To suppose that the Arabs, after living in isolation for centuries, could suddenly enter into the game of conducting 'wars of nerves' and overwhelmingly outsmart the British—that idea is preposterous. . . .

"The Arab League is just another Moscow-engineered false front organization. It is a convenient device whereby the Communists can create division and misunderstanding within the camp of the democracies. The Jews represent a powerful financial and political force in the democratic world. There can be neither unity nor strength in Christendom so long as the Gentile leaders of Britain (and America) yield to atheist-Moslem pressure to keep the Jews out of Palestine.

"The barring of the Jews from Palestine represents a serious compromise of all that democracy and Christianity stand for. The betrayal of the Jews is, in reality, a flat violation of Biblical teaching, which is the very foundation of the Anglo-Saxon concept of democracy. So long as the Jews are kept out of Palestine the cause of Christianity is made a mockery before all nations of the world. The 'four freedoms' appear a wicked snare so far as the Jews are concerned. Democracy itself is made to writhe in impotence and degradation in the face of world opinion and the conscience of mankind.

"Russia's age-old ambition is to establish her sway in the Mediterranean area. Through the Arab League, she has effectively embarrassed and undermined British prestige. . . ."

While Russia will have formidable allies in her encirclement and ultimate invasion of Palestine, the Arabs—curiously enough—do not figure prominently among them. In fact, Ezekiel plainly indicates that certain groups of Arabs will be numbered among the nations which will launch a final ";protest" against the Russian assault on Palestine. The nations which join in the "protest" against Russian aggression include "the merchants of Tarshish" (England) and "all the young lions thereof" (U. S. A., Canada, and Australia); also included are "Sheba and Dedan." *The International Standard Bible Encyclopedia* states: "Sheba was the name of an Arab tribe.' Davis' *Dictionary of the Bible* asserts that the Dedanites were "an important commercial people of Arabia."

Thus, we see that ultimately important groups of Arabs shake loose from the Moscow influence and join the nations arrayed against Russia. In view of this Scriptural fact, we see how extremely wide of the mark are the propagandists who represent the Palestine crisis as "a struggle between Arabs and Jews."

## WAR PREPARATIONS AGAINST PALESTINE

Who are the major allies of Russia in her assault upon Palestine? They are drawn from all three continents—Europe, Asia, and Africa. Preparatory to the attack on the Holy Land, the power of the North—Russia—forms one of the most formidable military organizations ever brought together on the face of the earth.

"Gomer and all his bands" become the European allies of Moscow. Gomer, of course, is Germany. Not many weeks ago, General Eisenhower mournfully conceded that Germany is being communized. Berlin is supposed to be under joint British-American and Russian control; but the Reds got there first, and established a prior hold on the city before the American-British forces were permitted entry. Clever communist propagandists have set in motion the processes of "total Bolshevization."

Next to General MacArthur, General Patton has been accredited with the deepest understanding of how to combat communism in a vanquished nation. But the influence of the Communists in Europe was well demonstrated when they forced the removal of Patton from his position of high command. The trumped-up charge was that Patton was "too easy on the Nazis." The true objection to him was that he was "too rough on the Reds;" that is, he refused to permit the Communists to put their hand-picked agents in the chief administrative posts. Ever since they "got" Patton, the Reds have been yammering for the removal of MacArthur, but so far they have not succeeded. So far, the Reds have been concentrating on China, rather than Japan, in the Asiatic theater.

Not only Germany, but all of central Europe has been swung under Moscow influence and control. Practically all the nations that formerly were occupied by the Nazis are now controlled by the Reds. The Nazis did a thorough job of sowing the seeds of anti-Semitism. The Communists are carefully cultivating the crop of "Jew-hate," which will be the ideological driving force of their aggressive war against Palestine.

Ezekiel lists "the house of Togarmah," along with "Gomer and all his bands," as European allies of the Palestine-bound Russian war machine. Dr. Rimmer, and others, assert that "the house of Togarmah" is Armenia. This writer's careful investigation leads him to believe that "the house of Togarmah" *includes* Armenia, but is assuredly not limited to that one little nation. It appears that "the house of Togarmah" embraces the whole Balkan area. The Balkan states, for the most part, are not laid out along "natural geographical lines." After every war, the habit has been to make "hamburger" of the Balkan states. They have been chopped up, amputated, engrafted, swollen or shrunken, as the case may be, to such an extent that all original or natural boundaries have long since been obliterated. It is self-evident that whatever power controls one of them will inevitably incorporate all of them under its domain. Both the Bible and current history demonstrate that Russia has definite and enduring designs upon the Balkans. In fact, she is now in process of gobbling the last of them up. The very area of Europe which is described as falling under Gog's control is now virtually all securely under the hegemony of Moscow. The European section of the military empire, formed in preparation for the attack on Palestine, is now practically entirely under Moscow rule.

The African and Asiatic allies of Russia have, for the most part, yet to be brought into the Bolshevik bear's camp. But he is making it plain that he means to have them—as allies and satellites.

The democratic world was stunned when Molotov, at the London foreign ministers' conference, flatly and boldly demanded for Russia the African colonies of Italy. The demand seemed preposterous—even incredible—in view of two factors: first, their remoteness from Russia; and, second, the failure (or, should we say, impossibility?) of Russia's participating actively in the fighting against Italy. America wants no colonies or loot out of the war, but neither France nor Britain have ever evidenced a lack of hungriness along this line. Even a pro-Soviet observer would have to concede that both England and France would have a better claim to the African colonies of Italy than would Russia.

But Molotov did not try to prove that Russia had any "right" to the colonies. He simply stated Stalin's insistence that they be handed over—with no questions asked or answers given! The request was denied in a heated session: which contributed to the break-up of the highly-ballyhooed London conference of the Allied foreign ministers. However, the Communist press loudly boasted that Russia would establish the footholds and strongholds she wanted in Africa, "one way or another." Internal revolution is the "other" way that Russia establishes her sway over coveted territory. She has played this game very cunningly in a number of nations in Europe. When Britain and America refuse to let her take over a nation bodily, she graciously joins with them in bestowing "democracy" upon the people. Soviet propagandists and terrorists then circulate among the people to insure a "soviet victory at the polls." The "elections" so far held in European nations adjacent to Russia have been the worst of farces; uniformly, they have resulted in the "election" of a totalitarian system of communist dictatorship. In the case of the Italian colonies in Africa, the communist method of seizing control will doubtless be that of outright revolution.

While the Molotov insistence that Russia must have the Italian colonies in Africa seemed strange and mystifying to Allied diplomats at the London conference, it is not at all surprising to the student of Ezekiels prophecy. *For, Ethiopia and Libya—the Italian satellites in the dark continent—are plainly listed among the allies of Russia in the foray against Palestine!* (Ezekiel 38:5)

## RUSSIAN AGGRESSION AGAINST PERSIA

Persia—once a world empire in her own right—is the principal Asiatic ally of Russia as she sweeps down upon the land and people of Palestine.

The clumsiest blunder ever made by the usually smooth-maneuvering Russian bear is apparent in the attempted Communist coup in Iran (Persia). It would seem that the Lord has caused Gog's foot to slip, in order that the half-blind democratic world might realize that Russia is building a European-African-Asiatic empire of just the dimensions described by Ezekiel, in preparation for the depredation of Palestine.

Doubtless, the Red conspirators intended the "Persian revolt" to have the appearance of a "spontaneous uprising of the natives," but the camouflage was flimsy to the point of transparency. In the first place, the "revolt" broke out in the very area of Iran occupied by Russian troops. The "Iranian revolutionists" are disclosed to be abundantly supplied with Russian guns and military equipment, while Red Army trucks transport them from one strategic spot to another to stage their "demonstrations."

Although the "revolt" has little support from the Iranian people, the government at Teheran dispatched troops to restore law and order. The Red Army, thereupon, blockaded the roads into the areas affected by the "revolt;" when the Iranian government's troops arrived, they were ordered by the Red Army high command to turn back. Apparently, the purpose of the Red Army in the occupied area is to insure the continuance of the "revolutionary reign of lawlessness."

A glance at the background of the Persian situation reveals that Gog must be drunk with power and hell-bent for conquest to go to the wild length of fostering such a makeshift, framed-up "revolt" as a means of solidifying communist control in Iran. Late in 1942, Great Britain, America, and Russia undertook a three-way occupation of Iran. As in Germany, each nation garrisoned troops in a separate area. *The purpose was to insure the full and uninterrupted flow of American lend-lease supplies to Russia.* The United States went all-out in modernizing Iran, building new railroads, highways, and harbors in order to supply Russia. When the war was over, Iran was given an immense amount of American material, all the way from locomotives and rolling stock down to harbor installations, trucks, airdromes, etc.

(There still are no new locomotives or rolling stock [railroad freight and passenger cars] for the United States. Returned soldiers and civilians must still stand up on trains! But, thanks to lend-lease, both Iran and Russia are abundantly supplied.)

Not only has the "revolt" been staged in the Russian zone of occupation, but the Red Army, taking advantage of trains and highways supplied by America, has sealed off this section of the nation with mobile "border patrols." The "revolt" is thus a Russian-staged show operating under "Red Army protection" in the Soviet theater of occupation.

In perpetrating such an outrage, it is clear that the Russians have no regard for either American or world opinion. With utter ruthlessness, they are pursuing the purpose of establishing permanent Communist dictatorship in Northern Persia. Undoubtedly, they will declare the "revolution" a success; and will install an "Iranian revolutionary regime" in power which will take orders direct from Moscow. Even if the present "revolt" should peter out before achieving this goal, the Soviets can be expected to follow-up with more severe "strong-arm" measures. Unless he thoroughly intended to establish Soviet sway in Persia, Gog would not have shocked and outraged world opinion by resorting to such ruthless tactics.

However the present bid for power turns out, whether Russia "brings Iran into camp" now or later on, the important thing is this: Moscow has brazenly made known its designs upon Persia. Russia has clearly evidenced that she will go to any length, resort to any crime against international law, indulge in any form of blackmailing and blackjacking, to gain control in Persia.

Iran may escape the clutches of the Soviet bear this time, but hardly next time! Persia is far from Britain and America, but next-door to Russia. America is in no mood to embark on a fresh military expedition; but if Uncle Sam were disposed to send substantial aid in any direction, it would be to the Christian government of China, fighting for survival against the Communist insurrectionists. It would hardly be to Persia! Britain, on the other hand, finds her forces spread very thin over her farflung empire. She could hardly send aid of any substantial sort to the Iranians.

Persia is doomed to be entrapped by the Russian bear. She is doomed to be captured and incorporated within his military empire, now in process of formation for the eventual foray against the land of Abraham.

(To fully understand the Soviet strategy in Iran, this "detail" should be noted: according to Anglo-Soviet agreement, all foreign troops are to be withdrawn by March 2, 1946. (The Americans are already gone.) After March 2, 1946, "Iranian independence and sovereignty" are supposed to be "recognized" by both Britain and Russia. Obviously, the Red purpose now is to install a Moscow-made revolutionary government of "native" puppets of Sovietism. Then, when the Russian troops are finally withdrawn a governing clique obedient to Moscow will be left behind. As in Poland and other Soviet-controlled puppet states, the "independent and sovereign" government which the Allies will "recognize" will be merely a tool for the enforcement of the Kremlin's rulership over a newly stolen empire, the formation and operation of which is clearly described by Ezekiel.)

## SOVIET ANTI-SEMITISM

Communist Russia is the most fiendish enemy of the Jews, yet it subtly pretends to be their friend and succeeds in deceiving many of them by its false propaganda. The Communists are also the deadly enemies of organized labor; under Communism, labor unions are abolished and the right to strike is denied. Yet, by pretending to be the friends of labor, the Reds have brought many branches of the C. I. O. and other groups to accept their deceptive and destructive leadership.

The Moscow dictatorship is motivated by the Satanic desire to frustrate the budding of the "fig tree." By keeping the Jews out of Palestine, the flowering or "fruiting" of the tree is obstructed. But an attack aimed at the roots of the tree has the same purpose: to make it barren. The Zionist-movement is designed to bear fruitage in Palestine, but it draws strength and vitality through its roots which maintain contact with the Jews of all parts of the world.

As it is with the Gentiles, some Jews are patriotic and some are seditious; some are democratic and some are Communistic; some are true to their fathers' faith and others are apostate and atheistic. In America and Britain, and other democratic nations, the atheistic-Communist Jews have been organized into a powerful anti-Zionist movement. Contrary to what some observers suppose, the Jews are not united behind the "back-to-Palestine" program. The Moscow-led element among the Jews is bitterly and violently opposed to Zionism.

The strategy of Communism is to offer a Satanic substitute for the promise and program of God. The Lord says: accept Me as Savior and I will provide you with a mansion in Heaven. The Reds scoff at Heaven as "the promise of pie in the sky;" they promise, "follow us and we will provide you with the good things of life here on earth." Communism offers an earthly utopia in place of a Heavenly home.

God's promise to Israel is that He will re-establish and resettle His people in the promised land of Palestine. The atheist-Communists scoff at God's promise. They counsel the Jews to turn their backs upon the Lord's provision for their future. By following the Red Flag of revolution, they contend that the Jews—along with the rest of mankind—can carve out a "promised land" of their own, can establish a worldly utopia in which human desire, not the Will of God, shall have full reign.

Every schoolboy knows that, historically and traditionally, Russia has been the most remorseless persecutor of the Jews. Long before the blight of anti-Semitism blacked out the culture and civilization of Germany, a favorite Russian pastime was the staging of anti-Jewish pogroms.

In a clever gesture to deceive the Jews, the Bolsheviks in 1920 enacted laws which were supposed to "guarantee" complete "racial equality." But, like their provisions for "religious liberty," these "laws" never had any meaning outside the official propaganda of the Moscow International.

In the struggle to attain power, the Bolsheviks accepted the cooperation of any Jews who would help them in overthrowing the Czar. Once Stalin came into power, however, at the death of Lenin, he began the blood purge of all Jews from the Communist Party. Even Leon Trotsky, Jewish partner of Lenin in leading the Revolution, was driven from the nation and finally murdered by Stalin's thugs in Mexico. Jews marked for extermination were officially labeled *"Trotskyites."* When the purge of Jews was extended throughout both the Communist bureaucracy and the Red Army, in the late nineteen thirties, the official charge was made that these political and military leaders were "guilty of conspiring with the Nazis." However, in 1939, Stalin himself entered into a full alliance with Hitler and signed the infamous Nazi-Soviet accord. So, if the unfortunate victims of the "purge" had made friends with the Nazis, it was obviously in line with Stalin's own policy! The fact, of course, is that they were "liquidated" as part of the program to rid the Bolshevik government of Jews.

In an article published in August, 1945, Solomon M. Schwarz presents complete evidence of the plague of anti-Semitism now sweeping Russia. One of the main reasons that the Soviets will not permit foreign observers or correspondents into their land; one of the main reasons for keeping Soviet Russia completely isolated from the rest of the world, is to conceal the anti-Semitic program now being carried out in the land of the Soviet.

Mr. Schwarz reports that, after the "purge," a new "ruling bureaucracy" was installed in Russia. "In the formation of the new social 'elites' an unmistakable trend, never openly acknowledged, was noticeable: Jews were systematically excluded from leading positions."

After the Soviet-Nazi pact of 1939, a wave of anti-Semitism swept over Russia. It is still rising to new and more intense heights. Mr. Schwarz explains, "Rumors about this new tide of anti-Semitism in Russia appeared about two years ago. These rumors were reported by refugees who had been permitted to leave the Soviet Union following various pacts with Allied nations. Now and then some news trickled through in private letters."

Even Jewish groups that were formerly pro-Soviet in their attitude are becoming alarmed at the outbursts of Soviet anti-Semitism. The English-language *Bulletin*, published in Palestine by the one group that has been consistently apologetic on behalf of Communist Russia, published an article in its March, 1945, issue, detailing the rise and spread of "wartime anti-Semitism" in Russia. This is what happened when the Nazis were driven out of Kharkov and the Jews streamed back to their homes: "The Ukrainians received the returning Jews with open animosity. During the first week after the liberation of Kharkov, no Jew ventured about alone in the streets at night. . . . In many cases, Jews were beaten in the marketplace. . . . In Kiev, sixteen Jews were killed in the course of a pogrom which took place after the murder of a Russian officer by a Christian woman who was believed to be a Jewess.

"The Jews returning to their homes received no more than

a small porportion of their property. Ukrainians summoned to court for possession of Jewish property were aided by other Ukrainians, who gave false evidence against the Jews.

"The Ukrainian authorities are greatly anti-Semitic. Applications by Jews are not treated properly. When the Commercial Academy moved from Kharkov to Kiev, several Jewish professors applied for permission to go there; but their applications were rejected. They addressed themselves to the chairman of the Ukrainian Soviet but received no response. The Jewish theater was not allowed to return to Kharkov, and broadcasts in Yiddish were not resumed."

In his article on Soviet anti-Semitism, Mr. Schwarz tells of the rampant and rampaging Jew-hate in the Red Army. In my book, *The End of Stalin—in the Light of Bible Prophecy* (35c from the publishers of this book), evidence is adduced to show that a military clique is rising to dominance in Russia. This clique is violently and bitterly anti-Jewish.

Authoritative reports from Russia disclose that even Jews who proved themselves heroes on the field of battle are treated with contempt upon their return home. Wounded Russian soldiers are scrutinized before being admitted to veterans' hospitals. Those who appear to be Jews are refused entry. The most pathetic beggars on the streets of Russian cities are disabled Jewish war veterans, for whom the Soviet government accepts absolutely no responsibility.

Mr. Schwarz tells of the mistreatment of Jews even when they volunteered for service in the "Soviet underground" during the German occupation. Jewish patriots formed a special "Jewish battalion." Even "the commanders were Jews and the language of command Yiddish." Despite the heroic and effective fighting of this battalion, the attitude of the Russian people, of other "underground" or partisan fighting units, and of the Red Army itself was uniformly "hostile." This Jewish battalion was hated even more intensely than were the Nazis. Finally, the Jewish battalion was stripped of its guns by army officials. A mob then descended upon the Jewish veterans "attacking them with scythes and whatever was at hand, and cutting them to pieces."

Mr. Schwarz then raises the question, "What was the official (government) reaction to this increase of anti-Semitism? Strangely, there wasn't any! During this period the Soviet press never raised the issue of anti-Semitism; it simply ignored it."

We can only conclude that silence meant assent. Indeed, there is strong evidence that the whole wave of anti-Semitism was "planned" by the Soviet government in Moscow. As Mr. Schwarz observes, "The silence of the Soviet press was not accidental. It was a policy adopted deliberately, and systematically carried out."

Official government agencies have reverted to the system of the most anti-Semitic of the Czars. *Jews are not counted as human beings, let alone citizens of Russia;* instead, they are enumerated and classified on a scale lower than the animals. While this may seem unbelievable, the facts demonstrate it to be true.

Murdering Jews is not counted a crime, even when it is done by the Germans! Listen to Mr. Schwarz: "In July, 1943, several Nazis were tried in Krasnodar for 'atrocities committed by the German-fascist occupants and their accomplices.' The trial lasted several days and was accompanied by the usual publicity. Reports of the proceedings were broadcast and published in all the newspapers; it was a big political show and was meant to be an example for the world. Yet neither in the indictment, nor in the summation of the public prosecutor, was there any allusion of the *systematic torture and mass execution of Jews.*"

Among the crimes charged against the Germans were the "burning of public buildings" and the "slaughter of pigs belonging to collective farms." (The penalty in Russia for "damaging government property" is death—whether the offender is a citizen or an alien.) But the slaughter of Jews is not considered an offense worth mentioning. Had the Germans confined their slaughter to Jews, leaving the Russians and the

Soviet buildings and state-owned pigs alone, there would have been no indictment leveled against them!

Mr. Schwarz informs us further, "When the Supreme Soviet of the Ukranian Republic convened on March 1, 1944, for the first time since the liberation of the Ukraine, Premier Nikita Khrushchov spoke at length on the sufferings of the population. He referred with deep emotion to the hundreds of thousands of the martyred and the slaughtered, to the terrible distress inflicted upon 'our people' during the occupation, *but not once did he mention the fact that a high percentage, and possibly the majority of these martyres were Jews.* It was not only the Ukraine that was now 'without Jews'; there was no room for them either in the lengthy speech of the head of the Ukrainian government." (Emphasis his.)

Not only in the Ukraine, but throughout Russia the fixed policy is pursued of regarding Jews as "non-human beings," who are not to be counted or considered even for statistical purposes. Investigator Schwarz reports, "Ever since the spring of 1944, Soviet newspapers have printed reports of the Special State Commission for the Investigation of Nazi Atrocities. On March 1, a report was published on the Kiev region; on May 7, the Rovno region; on June 14, the Odessa region. In these areas the Jews constituted a large part of the urban population; their agony and mass destruction was the outstanding feature of the Nazi crimes. *Yet there is not the slightest hint of this in the reports of the various Commissions, most of which do not inclued a single Jew as a member.*" (Emphasis his.)

In preparation for the "day of vengeance," the Soviets kept careful records of all individuals tortured, mistreated, or murdered by the Nazi invaders.*But no Jews are included among them!* In indicting the Germans for "crimes against humanity" only offenses against non-Jews are cited; apparently, Jews are not included as members of the human race, as constituents of humanity!

The Lithuanian Soviet Republic published a report on Nazi atrocities on December 20, 1944. Mr. Schwarz reports, "It lists and describes with meticulous accuracy the camps where thousands upon thousands of 'scientists and workers, engineers and students, Catholic and Orthodox priests, the inhabitants not only of Vilna, but also of other towns and villages of the Lithuanian Soviet Republic . . .', 'peaceful Soviet citizens from Kaunas . . .', and '. . . French, Austrian and Czechoslovak citizens . . .' met their deaths. *There is not a single word about Jews.*"

In its June, 1945, issue the Zionist magazine *Furrows* expressed "amazement" at the failure of the official Soviet film on the Maidanek concentration camp even to hint at the fact that most of the victims were Jews. It declares, "At this infernal spot, perhaps one-third of Polish Jewry was murdered in gas chambers and in furnaces."

Describing this official government film, which must reflect official Soviet policy of anti-Semitism, the magazine asserts: "Watching the picture one is overcome by an incomprehensible feeling that something is missing. Hundreds of thousands of Jews were murdered at Maidanek only because they were Jews. . . . In the picture none of this is even hinted at. The narrator speaks of Poles, Czechs, Greeks, Frenchmen, but he does not mention Jews once. The film shows a table covered with several passports; a Pole's, a Czech's, even a Greek's, but there is no passport of a Jew.

"Amazement gives way to a feeling of stupor and horror as the film nears its conclusion. The remains of thousands upon thousands are shown being interred in a field (in Poland). Most of them are Jewish, but a gigantic cross surrounded by Catholic priests and nuns is raised over the mass grave. A Catholic requiem resounds over the graves of the hundreds of thousands of Jews who only a few years ago prayed in the synagogues of Warsaw, Lublin, Cracow and other Polish cities."

The Nazi method of oppressing the Jew was to make him conspicuous. Like lepers, Jews under Nazi rule were obliged to wear badges proclaiming themselves to be contaminated and unclean: unfit for association with "Aryans." With characteristic German thoroughness, the Jews were branded, stigmatized, card-catalogued.

The Soviet method of oppressing the Jews is to make them *inconspicuous*. They are counted neither as citizens nor aliens. They are regarded as *non-entities*. It matters not what becomes of them: whether they live or die. A hundred thousand of them may perish in one gigantic massacre, but the fact is not even accorded official government "notice." Russian citizens or foreigners may rob, abuse, torture and murder Jews with impunity. Jews simply "do not exist," officially; therefore, a crime committed against them is not even recognized, noted, or recorded by government officials, let alone punished.

Even inmates of a prison are counted and numbered. But the Jews of Russia are uncounted, nameless, and unnumbered.

As a manifestation of their contempt for the Jews, the Nazis deliberately made them *conspicuous*. To show their contempt for the Jews, the Communists purposely make them *inconspicuous*. Which form of degradation is more cruel?

Whatever the answer may be, the Russian system is more subtle. Since official government documents never mention the life or death, abuse or torture, rape or murder of a Jew— there is no way that the outside world can ever know the extent of the pogroms, or the nature of the persecutions, against the Jews carried on inside Soviet Russia.

The Communists will continue loudly to ballyhoo their "international friendship for the Jews," while in the land of the Soviet the people of Israel are subjected to the most fiendish forms of mistreatment; and while, all the time, Gog is marshalling and mobilizing his military might, and that of his allies, for the visitation of his supreme hatred and scorn upon the land of Palestine itself.

# THE COMING CONFLICT

In viewing with regret the distressing record of Britain in failing to enforce the right of the Jews to reoccupy Palestine, we do not engage in any spirit of condemnation. Rather, our purpose is that, first of all, of attaining to full understanding of the British position.

In stirring the whole Mohammedan world in open or undercover revolt against the British, the Russian Communists have succeeded in putting John Bull very desperately and dangerously "on the spot."

When American-British forces landed in North Africa, Winston Churchill referred to this move as an attack to be leveled across the Mediterranean at the "soft underbelly" of Hitler's bristling European "fortress," as it was then called.

The "soft underbelly' is a section which is virtually unprotected, but which tabernacles the vital organs of the human body. In boxing bouts, "hitting below the belt" is the most grievous of fouls.

The "soft underbelly," of the British Empire coincides with the "Moslem world." Starting at Tangier, it spreads through the Mediterranean and North Africa, across the so-called Middle East to the Indian Ocean, across to Southeast Asia, and the islands of the South Pacific. Palestine is virtually the heart and center of this whole Moslem "belt."

This is the "great colonial zone of the world." It is also the main communication line of the British Empire. But the area includes vast expanses of the French and Dutch empires. Neither the French nor the Dutch are in a military position to defend their colonial empires. But for her own protection, Britain must hold them intact. Revolution, anarchy, or chaos in any part of this whole general area would create a spreading sore that would constitute a growing danger to the integrity of the British Empire itself.

Max Werner, famous analyst of affairs foreign and military, warns that Britain is beset by troubles and perils of small and large magnitude: "There are many potential colonial wars smouldering between Singapore and Gibraltar. . . . The belt. of tensions, unrest and semi-wars today spreads from China through Southeast Asia, the Indian Ocean, the Middle East and the Mediterranean to the Atlantic coasts of North Africa."

John Bull is sitting on a powder keg. It is true that many of the colonial tribes and peoples "do not possess industrial and military potential." But in the African wildernesses and the Asiatic wastelands, the native rebels can offer deadly and determined opposition even to a superior foe supplied with bombers and heavy artillery.

The real menace of the revolting Moslems, of course, derives from the undercover aid which they can count upon receiving from Moscow. Britain is very reluctant to crush "rebel resistance" when the Soviets stand behind it. Both America and Britain have been slow and feeble to offer effective assistance to our long-time ally, Chiang Kai-shek, as he battles to subdue the Communist rebels in China. The fear is openly expressed that we would come into conflict with Russia, if we offered substantial assistance to Chiang Kai-shek. It is true that the British have struck powerful blows to subdue the Indonesians, but there is little fear there of dire consequences coming from "antagonizing the Soviets," for the simple reason that there is no way that Russia could supply important quantities of armaments to the Indonesians, even if she were disposed to seek a showdown against the British in that area.

The situation is reversed in Persia, however, as we have pointed out. Britain cannot intervene decisively there from a military standpoint, and therefore has little choice but to abandon the country to the Soviets after the launching of "formal protests."

The same condition prevails, to a lesser degree, with respect to Palestine. Suppose the British had stood firmly upon a policy of "unrestricted Jewish immigration into Palestine?"

Suppose they had called the bluff of Moscow, which was using the troublesome Arabs as a buffer and blind? If a "showdown" had actually come, it is probable that the Soviets could have supplied arms both faster and in larger quantity to the Arabs than the British could have rushed them to their own forces and those of their allies. This, of course, is a highly speculative question. But the point is this: Britain backed down in Palestine, because of the obvious dangers involved in pursuing a course which would bring her into open clash with the Soviet-backed Moslem world.

Walter Lippmann, the renowned commentator on foreign affairs, believes that Prime Minister Attlee "retreated in Palestine" when he came to appreciate the shakiness and instability of the British position in the Moslem world. Like Messrs. Roosevelt and Truman, Attlee was elected on a platform which pledged him to establish immediate and unlimited freedom of Jewish immigration into Palestine.

Mr. Lippmann points out that "the British position is precarious" throughout "the whole Moslem world from Tripoli in the Mediterranean to the Netherlands Indies in the South Pacific." He argues, "Britain is deficient in the essential elements of authority—in prestige, in military power, and in capital resources. Her prestige is impaired by the rising tide of nationalism among the Moslem and Hindu peoples of North Africa and South Asia. The military power which the British Isles can maintain in that part of the world is exceedingly limited; as a matter of fact, Great Britain has to draw on India, as the affair in Java illustrates, for the troops which would be required if her authority were put severely to the test."

This all adds up to the conclusion, contends Lippmann, that Attlee was "not in a position to adopt the policy" and put it in effect *after election* which he championed so earnestly before election.

Mr. Lippmann goes on to maintain that, since America does not have the bases for military prestige in the Moslem world, "The President had no choice but to 'accede' to the view of the British government that 'it was not in a position to adopt the policy' he had recommended—namely to grant an additional 100,000 certificates for the immigration of Jews into Palestine."

We can understand the "reasoning" which is at the bottom of the decision made by Mr. Attlee and the advisers to President Truman. But on the basis of the Word of God, we must say most emphatically that it is neither sound nor convincing.

Perhaps it would have been "dangerous" for Britain to open up Palestine to the Jews in "defiance" of the "threats of violence" uttered by the Communist-incited Arabs. But it is a vastly more "dangerous" policy to keep Palestine closed in defiance of God's command that it shall be opened unto His people!

We do not question that Britain's position is "precarious" in the Moslem world; and that she might have brought herself into still graver jeopardy by disobeying the Soviet-Moslem demand: "Keep the Jews out of Palestine." But Britain is bringing herself into the greatest and gravest of all jeopardies by disobeying God's command: "Let My people return unto their own land."

Do British statesmen (and American ones, too) fear the Moscow-supported Arabs more than they fear Almighty God?

Granting the point that the British position is weak and shaky in the Moslem world, will it be made stronger by deliberate disobedience to God?

Nations are strengthened as they walk in the way and will of the Lord. Britain and America cannot find either safety or strength in the pursuit of any program which goes counter and contrary to God's Plan of the Ages. Peace and security can come to America and Britain *only* as we faithfully serve the Lord and His Great Purpose for Israel.

God's promise is still valid, and all history confirms it: He blesses those nations which are faithful and true to His Plan and Program for Israel; He visits wrath and judgment upon those nations which bring woe upon the people of Israel.

Hundreds of thousands of Jews will be hungry and homeless in Europe this winter, because America and Britain did not obey God's command that Palestine shall be opened up unto the people of Israel.

Neither Americans nor British want war or conflict with any people. But it is a vain and empty argument to contend that by "appeasing the Arabs," we have "averted bloodshed in the Holy Land."

There is peace only for the people who do God's Will: God's Will for Israel is that His people shall be relocated in Palestine. There is only war and the worst of woe for any nation which disobeys God and defies Him, while denying Palestine to His people.

Let us pray for those in authority in Britain and America. Let us pray that they shall be led to see the error of a policy which is contrary to the Will and Way of God, as revealed in His Own Word. Let us pray that America and Britain shall dedicate themselves to do the Will of God. on behalf of Israel.

Let us pray that our nation, and Great Britain, shall seek and find the way of true peace and security in the center of God's Will.

The Scriptures instruct us to pray for the peace of Israel. If America and Britain are to have peace, we must put the peace of Israel first. There can be no peace on this earth until the people of Israel dwell peacefully and safely in the land of Palestine.

Let us pray that our national leadership may have the courage and consecration to obey and follow God in our "Palestinian policy." True, this path may be "dangerous" and difficult. But any other path would involve infinitely worse "dangers" and difficulties, and would eventually lead us to the final disaster and destruction which await all nations and all peoples who turn their backs on God and His Word.

"The wicked shall be turned into hell, and all the nations that forget God."

## CHECK LIST OF DR. DAN GILBERT'S BOOKS ON
## BIBLE PROPHECY AND RELATED SUBJECTS

The Future of Britain and Bible Prophecy

The Future of Japan and Bible Prophecy

The Red Terror and Bible Prophecy

Mormonism Unmasked in the Light of Scripture

Hell Over Hollywood; the Truth About the Movies

What Really Went Wrong at Pearl Harbor?

Russia's Next Move

Is President Truman America's Man of Destiny?

The End of Stalin—in the Light of Bible Prophecy

One Minute Before Midnight

Who Will Be the Antichrist?

What Actually Happened to Hitler?

Any 3 of the above books: $1 (plus 4c for postage)

All 12 of the above books: $4 postpaid

---

Order from:

GENERAL BOOK AND BIBLE HOUSE
4800 South Hoover Street
Los Angeles 37, California

## CRUCIFYING CHRIST IN OUR COLLEGES

The book that has been more widely reviewed and discussed than any other book published in the twentieth century and dealing with a religious subject.

More than 150 leading religious magazines and newspapers, representing more than 80% of the total circulation of the religious press in America, have favorably commented upon this book.

Next to the church, the school is the most important agency in our country. Here is the evidence as to what is happening in the educational institutions of our nation. Here is the alarming proof of the growth and spread of anti-God influences in secular education.

Now in its 7th large edition, this book has made its deep impression upon the thinking of our times.

Every person who loves the cause of Christ will wish to know the facts set forth in this awakening volume.

Nearly 250 pages. Beautiful cloth binding.

**CRUCIFYING CHRIST IN OUR COLLEGES**

$1.50 per copy

———————

## THE MIND OF CHRIST

### What It Is

### and

### How to Possess It

The Bible tells us that the MIND OF CHRIST is God's gift to the believer.

The goal of every Christian should be to possess the MIND OF CHRIST, the WISDOM OF GOD.

The Bibel tells us how to THINK. It instructs us as to how to have POWER IN THOUGHT, IN CREATIVE INTELLECTUAL ENDEAVOR.

This book has been recommended by Christian psychologists as a most clear and practical setting forth of the Biblical principles of thought-power.

**THE MIND OF CHRIST**
**What It is and How to Possess It**
**Beautiful Cloth Binding**
$1.50 per copy

———————

```
GENERAL BOOK AND BIBLE HOUSE
4800 South Hoover Street
Los Angeles 37, California
```

## MODERNISM, COMMUNISM AND THE FEDERAL COUNCIL OF CHURCHES

Hundreds of thousands of dollars collected through leading denominational churches in America have been poured down the "rathole" of the Federal Council. This organization has become a leading agency for carrying on the war against fundamental Christianity and Constitutional Americanism.

The amazing truth about the Federal Council is set forth in books by Dr. Dan Gilbert.

### THE FEDERAL COUNCIL OF CHURCH AND BIBLE PROPHECY

This book demonstrates that the Federal Council was set up to serve a Satanic purpose. The Federal Council is preparing the way for the "world religion of Antiechrist." The Council is advancing the Great Apostasy—the program of treason against Christ and the Bible. Every charge is **proved**—on the basis of Scripture.

### THE FIFTH COLUMN IN OUR CHURCHES

This book brings together an amazing array of facts and figures. It shows how the Federal Council has carried on the most vicious undercover warfare against Bible Christianity. It contains material not previously put into print—to expose the activity of the enemies of God's Word.

Each of the above books: 35c per copy (plus 2c for postage)

---

## SPIRITUAL BOLSHEVISM
### The Truth About the Teachings of Jehovah's Witnesses

The fastest-growing Satanic cult in America is that of the miscalled Jehovah's Witnesses. Multitudes of our people have been led into the service of Satan's cause by the false and deceptive teachings of this destructive sect.

Hundreds of appeals have come from Christian pastors and workers in all parts of the country: GIVE US AMMUNITION TO USE AGAINST THESE PEDDLERS OF SUPERSTITION AND TREASON AGAINST GOD AND COUNTRY GIVE US THE TRUTH, THAT WE MAY MAKE IT KNOWN.

In response to these appeals, Dr. Dan Gilbert undertook to present the full facts regarding Jehovah's Witnesses. Trained in the profession of law, experienced in the field of journalism, Dr. Gilbert is highly qualified to UNCOVER the truth about the teachings of Jehovah's Witnesses, and then PRESENT this truth in the light of God's Word.

Dr. Gilbert's first book was entitled CRUCIFYING CHRIST IN OUR COLLEGES. In it, he dared to tell the truth about the anti-God teachings in our great universities. Even those who do not agree with him, admit that he has the COURAGE OF HIS CONVICTIONS.

Now, in his latest exposure of anti-God activity, he rips the mask from off the hideous false teachings of the WITNESSES. He shows that the WITNESSES secretly serve and salute the Red Flag of Moscow, even while they refuse to salute the American Flag. A book that will open your eyes. READ IT—DISTRIBUTE IT. Help to rescue the American people from the grip of Satan's special brand of superstition—RUSSELLISM.

### SPIRITUAL BOLSHEVISM